301
things to

Published by Bushel & Peck Books, a family-run publishing house in Fresno, California, that believes in uplifting children with the highest standards of art, music, literature, and ideas. Find beautiful books for gifted young minds at www.bushelandpeckbooks.com.

Type set in Didot and Tomarik Brush.
Cover visuals licensed from Shutterstock.com.

Bushel & Peck Books is dedicated to fighting illiteracy all over the world.
For every book we sell, we donate one to a child in need—book for book. To nominate a school or organization to receive free books, please visit www.bushelandpeckbooks.com.

ISBN: 9781952239564

First Edition

Printed in the United States

10 9 8 7 6 5 4 3 2 1

301
things to
DRAW

BUSHEL
& PECK
BOOKS™

WHEN PIGS REALLY DID FLY.

2

YOUR PRINCIPAL ON THE WEEKENDS.

THE WORLD'S LARGEST (AND QUITE POSSIBLY ONLY)
CITY MADE ENTIRELY FROM ICE CREAM.

4

A SPACE HOTEL.

A NOT-YET-DISCOVERED SPECIES OF DINOSAUR.

6

WHAT HAPPENED TO THAT DINOSAUR.

A TAP-DANCING GIRAFFE.

8

A DEVICE TO CATCH SANTA CLAUS.

WHAT THE EASTER BUNNY WORE ON HALLOWEEN.

10

SHAKESPEARE IN FOURTH GRADE.

AN ORANGUTAN TEACHING MATH (UNLESS THAT IS
YOUR TEACHER, THEN JUST DRAW HIM).

12

YOUR DREAM HOUSE.

A WIG MADE FROM NOODLES.

14

AN ELEPHANT WITH A PEANUT ALLERGY.

15

A MUMMY—UNWRAPPED.

16

A SUPERHERO WHO LOST HER POWERS.

A BUFFALO ABDUCTED BY ALIENS.

18

A DRINKING FOUNTAIN WITH PUNCH INSTEAD OF WATER.

THE EIFFEL TOWER BUILT WITH PRETZEL STICKS.

A BIRD WHO SWIMS INSTEAD OF FLIES.

A FISH WHO FLIES INSTEAD OF SWIMS.

22

A CIRCUS TRAIN.

SOMETHING AMAZING MADE FROM DUCT TAPE.

24

A CHRISTMAS CATASTROPHE.

THE SUN FIGHTING WITH THE MOON.

A NEW KIND OF BREAKFAST CEREAL.

THE LARGEST TELESCOPE EVER BUILT.

28

WHAT THAT TELESCOPE CAN SEE.

29

THE INSIDE OF AN ANTHILL.

A ZOO FULL OF HUMANS INSTEAD OF ANIMALS.

AN INTERGALACTIC DELIVERY MAN.

A PIZZA SHAPED LIKE YOUR FAVORITE STATE.

WHAT YOUR CROWN WOULD LOOK LIKE IF YOU WERE
KING OR QUEEN.

WHAT REALLY HAPPENS INSIDE THE SCHOOL KITCHEN.

THE SECRET WORLD INSIDE THE SEWERS.

36

THE PERSON YOU'D MOST LIKE TO MEET FROM HISTORY.

AN INVISIBLE CAR (GOOD LUCK).

A POLAR BEAR PLAYING CHECKERS WITH A RAPTOR.

A CHICKEN WHO BARELY CROSSED THE ROAD.

A SNOWMAN THAT RESEMBLES YOUR GREATEST HERO.

42

WHAT YOU'D MAKE IF YOU WERE ON THE GREAT
BRITISH BAKING SHOW.

A TV PLAYING YOUR FAVORITE CARTOON.

THE PHONE YOU WISH YOUR PARENTS WOULD GET
YOU (BUT PROBABLY WON'T).

45

A BABY LIFTING A CAR!

46

A RUNAWAY SHOPPING CART.

AN INCREDIBLE MINI GOLF COURSE.

THE HEADLESS HORSEMAN.

A CORN MAZE WITH ONLY ONE WAY OUT.

A POLICE CAR WITH DONUT TIRES.

A GENIE TRAPPED IN A BOTTLE.

WHAT'S ON THE OTHER SIDE OF THE RAINBOW.

A BRAND NEW MYTHICAL CREATURE.

A DENTIST CLEANING A DINOSAUR'S TEETH.

THE PERFECT SANDWICH.

A CANDY CANE FACTORY.

THE WORLD'S MOST IMPENETRABLE SNOW FORT!

58

A SAND DOLLAR.

WHERE THE TOOTH FAIRY STORES EVERYONE'S TEETH.

60

A COLONY ON MARS.

61

AN EPIC TREEHOUSE.

A PANDA NAPPING ON THE GREAT WALL OF CHINA.

A HOP-SCOTCH WITH 100 SQUARES.

WHAT WOULD HAPPEN IF BOOKS CAME TO LIFE.

YOUR SCHOOL BEING ATTACKED BY LLAMA NINJAS
(NUNCHUCKS OPTIONAL).

66

THE PLACE IN THE WORLD YOU MOST WANT TO VISIT.

A MAP FOR FINDING THE NORTH POLE.

A SPARKLY SEASHELL COLLECTION.

A RHINOCEROS BALLOON ANIMAL.

A PEACH DOING A HANDSTAND.

A GOLDFISH WHO OUTSMARTED A SHARK.

A PIRATE WITH A PET GOAT.

A TREE IN FOUR DIFFERENT SEASONS.

YOUR NEIGHBOR TAKING A RACCOON FOR A WALK.

A BOWLING ALLEY.

A MERMAID CASTLE.

A YAK WITH A BAD HAIR DAY.

WHAT REALLY HAPPENED TO THE GINGERBREAD MAN.

A BEAR MAKING SALMON ICE CREAM.

80

YOUR VERY OWN LOGO.

A BRAND NEW INSTRUMENT.

82

UNICORNS PLAYING RING TOSS.

A BOUQUET OF BUTTERFLIES.

84

A POT OF "EVERYTHING SOUP."

A HIPPO GOING DOWN A WATERSLIDE.

A BIKE MADE FOR THE SEVEN DWARVES.

BIRDS SPLASHING IN A BIRDBATH.

WHERE THE SQUIRRELS HID THEIR ACORNS.

89

A BEAVER CONTRACTOR.

THE WORLD'S FASTEST SLOTH.

A PONY SALON.

A MAGIC PENCIL THAT ALWAYS GETS THE RIGHT
ANSWER.

A CLOSE-UP OF YOUR HAND.

WHAT YOU HAD FOR BREAKFAST TODAY.

95

A SODA CAN.

A WATERMELON CUT IN HALF.

THE VIEW FROM YOUR WINDOW.

KING KONG VERSUS THE JOLLY GREEN GIANT.

A HOLIDAY WREATH.

A TRIPLE-DECKER IGLOO.

101

YOUR HOUSE INSIDE A SNOWGLOBE.

THE EARTH TAKING A BATH.

A BOOBY-TRAPPED BIRTHDAY PRESENT.

AN ANIMATRONIC GEORGE WASHINGTON.

A LEPRECHAUN.

A VERY COMPLICATED GUMBALL MACHINE.

A HALF-EATEN CHOCOLATE BAR.

108

A CAVEMAN USING A COMPUTER.

GLASSES THAT GIVE SOMEONE X-RAY VISION.

110

AN UNDERWATER ROLLERCOASTER.

MONEY THAT REALLY DOES GROW ON TREES.

WHAT YOU HOPE YOUR FIRST CHILD LOOKS LIKE.

YOUR PET'S PAW PRINTS.

A GLASS HALF EMPTY.

A GLASS HALF FULL.

A HURRICANE.

A SPACE TAXI.

A MONSTER DELIVERING PIZZAS.

119

A TRICERATOPS WHO WON'T STOP TALKING.

A ZUCCHINI ZOMBIE.

A YODELING CACTUS.

BEES WHO MAKE COTTON CANDY INSTEAD OF
HONEY.

RAINBOW ROSES.

A PICKLE PLAYING THE BANJO.

WHAT YOUR BATHROOM LOOKS LIKE ON OPPOSITE DAY.

A COW IN A TORNADO.

BURIED TREASURE!

A SUGAR-POWERED ICE CREAM TRUCK.

A DROOLING PUPPY.

A SELF-PORTRAIT.

A WALL COVERED IN GRAFFITI.

A PRINCESS FIGHTING A DRAGON—AND WINNING.

A CAVE.

A COMPUTER VIRUS.

A HORSE ON A UNICYCLE.

WHERE YOU LIVE.

A SUBSTITUTE TEACHER.

A TRAP TO CATCH THE EASTER BUNNY.

WHAT ABRAHAM LINCOLN WOULD LOOK LIKE TODAY.

140

THE WORLD'S MOST FAMOUS DIAMOND.

A SKATE PARK.

THE MOST INTRICATE SNOWFLAKE.

WHAT EGYPTIAN PHARAOHS DID FOR FUN.

A GRANDFATHER CLOCK.

A WARTHOG FLYING FROM A GIANT SLINGSHOT.

A GENIUS GRASSHOPPER.

AN INVENTION TO CURE BALDNESS.

AN ANT SAILING IN A PUDDLE.

AN AUTOMATIC POTATO PEELER.

A BUSINESS YOU'D WANT TO OPEN.

A KNIGHT LOST IN THE WOODS.

A BAGEL SHAPED LIKE YOUR LEFT EAR.

AN "ELEPHANT CROSSING" SIGN.

A FAMILY OF CHIPMUNKS.

A POCKET KNIFE THAT INCLUDES A BOTTLE OPENER, PANCAKE TURNER, TELEVISION REMOTE, AND GOLF CLUB.

A MISCHIEVOUS LAWN GNOME.

A VAMPIRE HIDING FROM THE SUN.

A YETI APPLYING TO WORK AT MCDONALD'S.

A TICKET TO A MOVIE YOU REALLY WANT TO SEE!

A BANK ACCOUNT WITH A MILLION DOLLARS.

A PROFESSOR OF MAGIC.

MILK AND COOKIES.

WHAT A HICCUP WOULD LOOK LIKE IF IT WERE A CREATURE.

164

A POSTMAN DELIVERING A LIVE TIGER.

A BOMB MADE FROM TOOTHPASTE.

WHAT IT WOULD BE LIKE HAVING THE ENERGIZER
BUNNY AS A PET.

THOR'S HAMMER.

168

THE WICKED WITCH OF THE WEST IN A FASHION SHOW.

YOU GETTING SHOT OUT OF A CANNON. WHOOPEE!

A LOBSTER RUNNING FOR PRESIDENT.

A HOLE TO CHINA.

172

A GOLDMINE.

PIGEONS PUTTING ON A PERFORMANCE OF ROMEO
AND JULIET.

CHICKENS WHO LAY SCRAMBLED EGGS.

AN ALLIGATOR DRIVING AN AMBULANCE.

A SWORD DECORATED IN GEMS.

A COMPLICATED MOUSE TRAP.

A BILLBOARD FOR A CHINESE RESTAURANT.

WHAT HAPPENS INSIDE A VENDING MACHINE.

YOU AS PRESIDENT OF THE UNITED STATES.

THE PRIZE SOMEONE FOUND IN THEIR CRACKER JACKS.

A NEW UNIFORM FOR YOUR FAVORITE SPORT'S TEAM.

183

A POSITIVE NUMBER WHO'S ACTUALLY QUITE GRUMPY.

184

A STONE-AGE CALCULATOR.

WHAT YOU REALLY, REALLY, REALLY WANT ON YOUR
BIRTHDAY.

A LION EATING ONLY SALAD.

A LADDER ALL THE WAY TO THE MOON.

A SECRET TUNNEL . . . AND WHERE IT LEADS TO.

A PERSON WINNING JEOPARDY.

A MINIATURE NAVAL WAR HAPPENING IN YOUR
BATHTUB.

WHAT A MICROSCOPE WOULD SEE ON YOUR FINGERNAIL.

A TYRANNOSAURUS SLIPPING ON A BANANA PEEL.

A NEWLY INVENTED BAND AID THAT DOESN'T HURT!

A HOT AIR BALLOON SHAPED LIKE CHEESE.

195

A TRAIN THAT GOES TO THE CENTER OF THE EARTH.

196

THE THING TAPPING ON YOUR CLASSROOM WINDOW

. . .

THE PRESIDENT ON HIS OR HER DAY OFF.

198

WHAT YOU'D SEE IN A MAGIC MIRROR.

THE BACK OF YOUR HAND (WHICH MOST PEOPLE
DON'T ACTUALLY KNOW THAT WELL).

THE MENU AT A RESTAURANT FOR WITCHES.

WHAT THE SPIDER ACCIDENTALLY CAUGHT IN ITS WEB.

MONKEYS WHO FOUND YOUR MOM'S MAKEUP.

A DOG CHASING HIS TAIL.

WHAT KINDNESS LOOKS LIKE TO YOU.

HOW THE PRISONER ESCAPED FROM JAIL.

AN OLYMPIC MEDAL.

WHAT YOUR SHADOW DOES WHILE YOU SLEEP.

A MACHINE THAT MAKES PAPER.

A COOKING SHOW.

210

A GIANT MAGNET—AND WHAT STUCK TO IT.

PLANS FOR A JEWELRY HEIST.

WHAT YOU WANT TO BE WHEN YOU GROW UP.

WHAT THE SUBMARINE SAW THROUGH ITS PERISCOPE.

A CAR DRIVING THE WRONG WAY.

A TURTLE RUNNING A RACE.

CANDYLAND.

CINDERELLA'S COACH.

A PIRATE HIDEOUT.

SATURN PLAYING UNO WITH JUPITER.

A FOOTBALL HELMET FOR YOUR FAVORITE TEAM.

221

WHAT YOU WANT FOR DINNER TOMORROW. BON
APPETIT!

THE GATE TO A HAUNTED MANSION.

A BANQUET FOR A GIANT.

THE TREASURE YOU FOUND IN A LOST TEMPLE.

A CUPCAKE BAKERY.

LIPSTICK ON A PIG.

227

A VENUS FLYTRAP.

A PERFECT BULLSEYE.

A SATELLITE IN SPACE.

230

A DONKEY IN A TUXEDO.

FRANKENSTEIN'S BRIDE.

A BRIDGE ACROSS THE GRAND CANYON.

A BOOKWORM.

A WINDMILL.

SIX FACES WITH SIX DIFFERENT EMOTIONS.

236

A TWO-STORY TENT.

INSTRUCTIONS FOR HOW TO MAKE A PEANUT
BUTTER AND JELLY SANDWICH.

A SUMO WRESTLER WALKING A TIGHTROPE.

YOUR SIGNATURE SEVEN DIFFERENT WAYS.

A MUG FOR YOUR FAVORITE TEACHER.

A TREE THAT GROWS FIVE DIFFERENT KINDS OF
FRUIT.

242

A PANCAKE THAT LOOKS LIKE BIGFOOT.

A SET OF SHOES FOR A CENTIPEDE.

A TOASTER THAT DOES MORE THAN MAKE TOAST (YOU DECIDE WHAT!).

WHAT COURAGE LOOKS LIKE.

A SHIP THAT COULD TAKE YOU TO MARS.

A POTION THAT GIVES YOU SUPER STRENGTH.

A TIME MACHINE.

A DISH YOU COULD MAKE OUT OF EGGS.

THE FIRST PET YOU EVER HAD.

A CLIMBER WHO REACHED THE TOP OF A MOUNTAIN.

252

A NEW WRAPPER FOR A CHOCOLATE BAR.

A PICNIC BASKET FILLED WITH YOUR FAVORITE
TREATS.

A FORTRESS MADE FROM ALPHABET BLOCKS.

A SINGING VOLCANO.

256

A COW WHO QUACKS AND A DUCK WHO MOOS.

A MAD SCIENTIST'S LABORATORY.

WHAT YOU WOULD MAKE FROM A CARDBOARD BOX.

A FLYING CAR.

260

A PARADE!

WHAT YOU WISH SCHOOL BUSES REALLY LOOKED LIKE.

YOU INSIDE YOUR FAVORITE VIDEO GAME.

WHAT YOUR HOUSE WOULD LOOK LIKE UNDER FIVE FEET OF SNOW.

A TOY MUSEUM.

SQUARE DANCING SKELETONS.

A BUNCH OF BALLOONS—AND WHAT THEY CARRIED AWAY.

YOUR FAVORITE CELEBRITY WALKING THE RED CARPET.

A LUMBERJACK.

AN ANGRY MOVIE DIRECTOR.

SHOES THAT MAKE YOU FLY!

271

AN X-RAY OF A SNAIL.

272

A PYRAMID BUILT UPSIDE DOWN.

A GRILLED CHEESE SANDWICH.

A FAIRY'S HOUSE.

A SECRET CAVE BEHIND A WATERFALL.

WHAT AN APPLE LOOKS LIKE THROUGH A FLY'S EYES.

A KEY TO A TREASURE CHEST.

AN EXPLOSION CAUSED BY 1,000 STICKS OF
DYNAMITE.

JACK'S BEANSTALK.

A FREEZE RAY GUN.

A TRAMPOLINE MADE FROM JELLO.

A FLEA CIRCUS.

THREE FOODS THAT START WITH M.

A CONSTELLATION THAT LOOKS LIKE AN OUTHOUSE.

A DREAMCATCHER.

A FACTORY THAT MAKES MARSHMALLOWS.

A ROBOT BUTLER NAMED JEEVES.

WHAT YOU'D DO WITH A MILLION DOLLARS.

A TINY BOAT MADE FROM LEAVES.

THE REASON YOU DIDN'T DO YOUR HOMEWORK.

291

A VEGETABLE GARDEN.

A WINDING ROAD.

THE LEANING TOWER OF "PIZZA."

THE WILDEST SOCKS EVER.

A BIRDHOUSE CONDOMINIUM.

A MAGIC TRICK.

YOUR GRANDMOTHER'S FALSE TEETH.

298

LEFTOVERS WHO CAME TO LIFE!

RAINING CATS AND DOGS—LITERALLY.

A BRAND NEW COIN (WITH YOUR FACE, OF COURSE).

A WHALE BRUSHING HER TEETH—ER, BALEEN.

ABOUT BUSHEL & PECK BOOKS

Bushel & Peck Books is a children's publishing house with a special mission. Through our Book-for-Book Promise™, we donate one book to kids in need for every book we sell. Our beautiful books are given to kids through schools, libraries, local neighborhoods, shelters, nonprofits, and also to many selfless organizations that are working hard to make a difference. So thank you for purchasing this book! Because of you, another book will make its way into the hands of a child who needs it most.

NOMINATE A SCHOOL OR ORGANIZATION TO RECEIVE FREE BOOKS

Do you know a school, library, or organization that could use some free books for their kids? We'd love to help! Please fill out the nomination form on our website (see below), and we'll do everything we can to make something happen.

 www.bushelandpeckbooks.com/pages/
nominate-a-school-or-organization

 If you liked this book, please leave a review online at your favorite retailer. Honest reviews spread the word about Bushel & Peck—and help us make better books, too!

Printed in the United States
by Baker & Taylor Publisher Services